Rival Claims for the Soul of Africa

Islam
Christianity
African Traditional Religions
Western Secularism

Patrick Wanakuta Baraza

Rival Claims for the Soul of Africa
Published by TurnKey Press
PO Box 80107
Austin, Texas 78758

For more information about our books, please write to us, call
512.478.2028, or visit our website at www.turnkeypress.net.

Library of Congress Control Number: 2007931844

ISBN-13: 978-1-934454-02-2
ISBN-10: 1-934454-02-8

TurnKey
press

In loving tribute to
My mother, Sabina Nelima
Who showed me the way to school.

Acknowledgments

This concise book belongs to many others, as much as to me. Literally every page contains the traces of encounters, both small and large – a conversation with a friend, a remark by an elder, a reader's suggestion, someone else's enthused writing on a particular subject, and, needless to say, a multitude of experiences with my people, the Bukusu of Western Kenya. Words are unable to express my profound appreciation to all those who have supported me and enriched the text.

Table of Contents

Prologue

To Tell the Lion's Tale...

A father entertained his young son with exciting stories about the conquests of hunters chasing after the lion. Puzzled, his son inquired "If the lion is supposed to be the king of the jungle, why is it that the hunter always wins?" The father responded, "The hunter will always win until the lion writes its own story."[1]

The peoples of Africa are heirs to three major types of religious tradition: African Traditional Religions, Christianity and Islam. The spiritual traditions of a people are part of their treasure. It is not wise to entrust the treasures of one people to another, for the greed of the one often leads to the abuse of the other; however, the spiritual treasures of African people have been historically misappropriated, misunderstood or misinterpreted, particularly by people of European and American descent.

A native African pours a libation on an ancestral grave in traditional veneration. A foreigner labels the act as ancestor worship, animism or fetishism. But the African believes that the ritual act of pouring a libation honors his ancestral spirits and the spirits of his living dead.

It is crucial for the scholar of Africa to understand and appreciate African spiritual history and experience, because a people or nation cannot be understood or appreciated without it.

Thesis of the Lion's Tale

This book examines the major themes of African Traditional Religions, summarizes religious thought and practices as manifested in Africa today, and discusses the effects on African people of the historical confluence of African Traditional Religions, Christianity, Islam, and to a lesser extent, Western secularism. The author also proposes avenues for dialogue among the major religions competing for the soul of Africa.

Religion and cultural practices make their way past generations through storytelling. Today, as for ages past, Africans are storytellers. Primarily oral people, they enshrine their history, cultures, religions, worldview, and values in stories, arts, and music. African oral arts are rich, diverse, living, and evolving. They entertain, inform, instruct, support, preserve, and reinforce the essential beliefs of African cultures. In the words of the Nigerian writer Chinua Achebe:

… It is only the story that can continue beyond the war and the warrior. It is the story that outlives the sound of war-drums and the exploits of brave fighters. It is the story…that saves our progeny from blundering like blind beggars into the spikes of the cactus fence. The story is our escort; without it we are blind. Does the blind man own his escort? No, neither do we the story; rather it is the story that owns us and directs us. It is the thing that makes us different from cattle; it is the mark on the face that sets one people apart from their neighbors.[2]

The story of traditional African religions and cultures must be told by a "Lion of Africa;" that is, by an African who knows through direct, lived experience the history and the spirit of African cultures and religions.

The Author's Story

I was raised according to traditional African religious practices in Kenya, as a member of the *Bukusu* tribe. As a youth I lived with my Muslim grandfather, while receiving a Christian education from Irish

Catholic missionaries. Consequently, I claim a triple heritage: African Traditional Religions, Christianity and Islam. Each provided me, and continues to provide generations of my people, with guidelines for conduct and solutions to life's challenges. From the time of my youth, I have witnessed how these religious traditions conflict in their attempts to shape the lives and cultures of African people.

The Catholic faith captured my soul in a most untraditional way. One day as a little boy, I was herding cattle along the foothills of Mount Elgon with several other boys, a daily chore in my tribal village in western Kenya. A Volkswagen Beetle drove up and a tall Irish priest got out, needing directions to the place where people would soon gather for the first Mass in our remote village. I volunteered to show him, and was invited to ride along in the Volkswagen. It was my first time in a car! After that, each time Father Tom Smith came to celebrate Mass in our village, he always asked after me. One day Father Smith asked, "Would you like to become a priest like me?" I responded, "If I become a priest like you, will I drive a Volkswagen?" Father Smith nodded, "Yes." Thus cemented my attraction to Catholicism! I completed a catechism program and was baptized in 1968, at the age of thirteen.

Years later, after attending seminary in Nairobi, I was ordained into the Catholic priesthood. A few days afterward, I was invited to the bishop's house. He talked with me and quizzed me on church doctrine. Then he took me outside, led me behind his house, and gave me the keys to an old Volkswagen Beetle. My priestly vocation was launched. If, as I believe, God speaks to us through the things we see and touch, then to a young boy in rural Africa, that Volkswagen was like God shouting in my ear.

As a young priest, I lived and worked with the *Pokot* people in the Rift Valley of northwest Kenya from 1985 to 1992. The Pokots are an isolated, nomadic tribe representing the poorest of the poor in my country; they travel as far as Uganda, Sudan, and Ethiopia in search of food and water for themselves and their animals.

After eight years of ministering to the Pokot people, a village tragedy changed the direction of my life. One evening, some women came running to my tent to tell me that a hand-dug well had collapsed and killed three young girls. According to Pokot tradition, dead bodies are abandoned to the hyenas. Despite this, and with the begrudging approval of their parents, I chose to lead a Christian burial service for these girls who were my close friends and newly baptized Catholics. Shattered, I left Pokot land and went to my bishop to discuss my future.

I wanted to further my education, preferably outside of Kenya. After researching various options, I chose the University of California, Berkeley, intending to study the traditions and cultures of African tribes. Of particular interest to me were the diverse African rites of passage. During the course of my studies, I came to realize how compellingly these African rituals, so familiar to me, communicated African cultural values, including ways of thinking and feelings. Through their rituals, my family, my clan, and my tribe preserved a culture, a worldview for future generations. Their rituals were building community. I learned that in his tribal religious practices the African affirmed, "I am because we are; and since we are, therefore I am."

Studying Islam at Berkeley

At Berkeley I delved more deeply into my Islamic heritage, for two important reasons. I wished to better understand Islam, especially because of my grandfather, who became a Muslim while serving in the British army in Burma during World War I, and who faced lifelong discrimination in our rural community, where Islam was unknown. Secondly, as Islam is the world's fastest growing religion, and particularly so in Africa, it is important to me as an individual, as well as to my tribal community and to the Kenyan Catholic community.

Reflections on My Berkeley Experience

My journey halfway around the world to study at Berkeley was the first step on a new path of my faith journey, a step with which my eyes were opened to a world of diversity. In Kenya, I experienced life in the tightly knit social fabric of a tribal family, in which extended families live and die together in a small geographical area. At Berkeley, I was introduced to new religions and cultural experiences, of the sort to which I would never have been exposed in my own country. At the University of California, Berkeley and in the Graduate Theological Union, I enriched both my Christian and Islamic heritage. I arrived at

Berkeley with a closed fist, but left with my hands open. I wish now to be passionately involved in the ministry of teaching others in America, and in my beloved Africa, what I have experienced and come to know about my homeland. I want to cry out about my country, to tell the Lion's Tale of Africa.

Adinkra Symbol for the Supremacy of God

CHAPTER I

Confluence of African Religions
The Lion's Tale Continues...

Long before Islam or Christianity arrived on African soil, Africa was at worship, its sons and daughters at prayer. There is no agreement on a name for these multifarious religious expressions. Some Western scholars have labeled all African religions under the blanket term, animism. Others use the singular reference, African Traditional Religion. This text will refer to the plural term African Traditional Religions, because they are neither monolithic nor homogeneous, but describe many cultures and languages.

As old as African civilization itself, African religious practices are defined and influenced by the language, geographical location, and culture of their practicing adherents. Tribal religious rituals and rites of passage reflect a people's beliefs about God, spirits, ancestors and the hereafter. There are over one thousand tribes south of the Sahara, each with its own religious structure and inherited system of meanings.

The Concept of God

Western metaphysical terms relating to God do not translate to the African way of thinking or speaking about God. Anyone using Western religious terminology in relation to African Traditional Religions is speaking an unknown language to his African audience. As one scholar explains, "African people may describe their deities as strong but not omnipotent; wise but not omniscient, old but not eternal, great but not omnipresent." [1] African deities written about in Western books, clothed with the attributes of a Christian God, are beyond the comprehension of the ordinary African in his village.

All indigenous African religions have a concept of a centralized divinity; that is, God is everywhere, all the time. God is not on "cloud nine" or on a throne, in recognizable human form. Rather, God is a spirit. One of the most explicit accounts of God as spirit is found among the Pygmy people of the Congo forest who say:

In the beginning was God,
Today is God,
Tomorrow will be God.
Who can make an image of God?
He has no body, He is a word
Which comes out of your mouth
That word! It is no more,
It is past and still it lives!
So is God. [2]

God the Father, God the Mother

Within the African frame of reference, God cannot only be the father. When told that God is the father, an African child will ask, "who is my mother?" In traditional African thinking, a father loves his children differently from a mother. A father loves his children chiefly because of their productive capacity in the tribe's benefit; a mother loves her children simply because they are her children. African prisons demonstrate this family dynamic. Prisoners are seldom visited by their fathers, and fathers are sometimes so ashamed of their criminal child that they change the family name. Nevertheless, mothers visit their imprisoned children, disregarding even public opinion rather than turning from part of their family. In the African family paradigm, both types of love, father and mother, are necessary for a healthy balanced life. God is father-mother. Everyone is brother and sister. God and humanity are family.

For traditional African people, the universe is the autobiography of God. The universe and all the forces of life are all manifestations of God. African people associate God with natural phenomenon; for example, the sky. In African languages, there are many names for God which also mean sky, heaven or above. The *Bari* or *Fujula* people of Sudan use the term *Ngu Lo Ki,* which means "God in the sky." The Pokot people of western Kenya call God *Tororot,* which is also their word for sky. The *Turkana* people of northwestern Kenya call God *Akuj,* meaning up above.

Rain is for the African people one of the greatest blessings. For that reason, God is commonly referred to as the *rain giver.* Similarly, thunder is understood as God's voice by many African people, such as the *Bavenda, Ewe* and *Ila* people of Congo. The *Kikuyu* of Kenya say, *"Ngai* (God) is cracking his joints" when thunder explodes, or that God is "talking to his people" in thunder and we should listen in silence.

Africans invoke God many times daily. They do so when they greet each other, when they discuss health matters or happiness, and when they wish each other goodbye. Among the *Banyarwanda* of Rwanda, when two people are parting, one says, "go with God," to which the other responds, "stay with God." One also hears, "may God go with you," or "may God make your feet light," for some one going on safari. A childless couple is greeted with "God give you fruit," or "God preserve you and keep you until you see your children's children." Such salutations, greetings, and farewells are prayerfully employed.

Centrality of Humanity

At heart of all traditional African religions is the fundamental belief that the purpose and value of any particular object in the universe is determined by its usefulness for human beings. Consider this mythological account of creation: The *Bukusu* people of western Kenya say that when God had created the sun, he wondered for whom it would shine. So God made the first man, and called him *Mwambu.* Since the man could talk and see, he needed a companion, and so God made the first woman, whose name was *Sela*. They wanted something to drink, so God made water fall from heaven, which filled up the holes and valleys to make lakes and rivers. God instructed *Mwambu* and *Sela* about the flesh they could eat. Some animals were allowed for food, while others were taboo. In this creation myth, humanity is at the very center of existence. The welfare of humanity is central. The diagram below, by John S. Mbiti, explains this belief, common to African Traditional Religions.

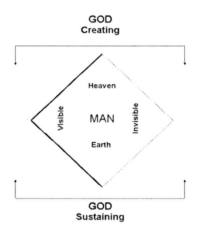

Man may be the center of the universe, but he is not its master. He is the friend, beneficiary, and user of a universe created by God. The universe is divided into visible and invisible parts; respectively, the earth and the heaven. Human beings are the link between the visible and invisible. Man is the priest of the universe. God is the creator and sustainer of the universe, the one who guarantees its continuity and harmony. Man's task is to observe the universe, to listen and respond to it, and most importantly, to create harmony with the universe—to reconcile the visible and invisible, which are God and humankind. Man selects parts of the universe as sacred, which reminds him that the entire universe is religious; in other words, to the African, his environment is a reflection of his religious beliefs—Mount Kiliman-jaro is more than a mountain, it is a religious phenomenon; it is God personified. From the African perspective, the whole world exists for

Man's sake. This worldview is deeply engrained in African people. It is the core traditional theology which dominates their creeds, moral teachings, and worship practices.

The Western Heaven and the African Zamani

To an African, even heaven exists for the purpose of humanity; there is no other reality in African thought. As explained by Okot P'Bitek, professor of anthropology at the University of Nairobi, African religions are "not grounded on a promise or a threat by some God that good people will, in the hereafter, enjoy life in heaven, while the bad will cook in the great fire."[3] By this he meant that for Africans, heaven is part of the tangible world. Furthermore, there is no place like the Christian hell where people are punished. Rather, people are punished and rewarded here on earth, in this life, a concept expressed by the *Banyarwanda* people of Burundi in their proverb: "God exercises vengeance in silence." Because he is concerned with the moral welfare of humankind, God defends morality and takes punitive action in the present.

Instead of a Western concept of heaven, African Traditional Religions refer to the *zamani*, a timeless place beyond which nothing can go. It is not thought of as being above the earth, as is so often the case in Western Christianity, but as below. One is thought to sink into the zamani from the *sasa* of the present time and place. Like the *dreamtime* of Australian Aborigines, "the zamani is the ocean of time in which everything becomes absorbed into the one reality that is neither after nor before."[4] All the wisdom of the ancestors and traditions of the people are held in the zamani. It is the final storehouse for all phenomena and events. It is the home of the spirits which can be entered only after death, and after *sasa* (now), which comprises not only physical life, but continued life in the memories of one's descendents.

The principal spiritual guides for African behavior are the ancestral founders of families, tribes and nations. The ancestors are the guardians of family and community affairs, tribal traditions, ethics, and activities. Having once lived on earth, the ancestors are familiar with the issues of human life, and serve as spiritual guides. They are available to teach, admonish, counsel and motivate their descendents to lead a good life and to bear children. They are remembered and honored through sacrifices, offerings, and the pouring of libations on their graves.

A unique group of ancestors are those who never lived the earthly human life, but nevertheless are spiritual guides. Among the *Shilluk* people of Sudan, there is this myth about an ancestor created by God:

The founder of the Shilluk royal house, *Nyikang*, was a son of a man who came from heaven, or perhaps was a being specially created in the form of a cow. ...he married a woman who was a crocodile, or a river creature that had the attributes of a crocodile, though as the myth develops she appears as a woman. This crocodile woman represents all the beings of the rivers, and offerings are still made to her at grassy spots where on the river banks crocodiles emerge. She is regarded as the patron of birth and protector of babies.[5]

Sacrifice to the ancestors continues to be common practice among Africans. In ancestral veneration, an animal is slaughtered upon the occurrence of a funeral, circumcision, marriage feast, or the birth of a child, and in times of illness.

The rituals and the language of the ancestors are deeply embedded in local African cultures. Ancestors abide in the zamani, which is the collective immortality, and they bear close relationships with humans; they are the doorway to the spirit world, which is real and present to the African. Hence, language describing the presence or reality of God or the spirit world is innate in African philosophy. Predating the advent of Christianity and Islam in Africa, ancestral veneration is the cornerstone of African religious consciousness, the basis of African spirituality.

The Rites of Initiation

African Traditional Religions incorporate rite of passage rituals, enacted in villages, through which young people are initiated into adulthood. The young initiates revere the wisdom of age, submitting themselves to traditional teachings as explained by the elders or village leaders. These rituals differ from one place to another. In most African tribes, preadolescent children are taught by their mothers and fathers, at home. Most tribes pass on their heritage to adolescents in seclusion. The ritual ceremonies mark the end of puberty and the beginning of adulthood.

Initiation rites are the tools for passing on tribal and cultural knowledge. These highly esteemed and respected rituals serve to train a child in traditional ethics, law and order, the prohibition of certain things that are taboo, respect for one's elders, home economics, the art of being a warrior, farming techniques, fishing, hunting, raising cattle, building houses, caring for the sick and the elderly, and many other community responsibilities.

The author personally underwent traditional African circumcision rites at the age of twelve. Among the *Bukusu* of western Kenya, the circumcision rite takes place every other year, in August. The actual date is announced three months before the ceremony. Candidates personally visit relatives and invite them to participate in the ritual ceremonies; no one would think of merely sending a letter or inviting anyone by telephone!

Accompanied by many young people, singing and dancing, I visited fifty families to invite them to the occasion. The circumcision took place very early in the morning, after the ceremonial washing at the river. I came back home naked, my body adorned with clay. I was in what might be called the *liminal* stage of my life, the threshold between an animal and a human being; that is, I was on the verge of psychological change. A very sharp, special knife was used. Though the operation was painful, I was encouraged to endure the pain without crying or shouting, or even showing a sign of fear. It was commonly held that if I cried or showed weakness, my mother would die, or no woman would marry me.

Following circumcision, the initiates are moved into a tribal isolation called *likombe*, during which time tribal elders instruct in tribal matters and teachings, some of which is utterly confidential, even to one's parents or spouse. In the course of his healing, relatives and friends of the newly circumcised bring gifts to the initiate in the form of money, ornaments, chickens and other animals. After three months, the young man leaves seclusion and returns home a new person, no longer a child, but an adult ready to assume community responsibilities, as directed by the elders.

Very often in literature, circumcision is portrayed as only a surgical procedure—an inadequate meaning in the African context. For the African, the primary purpose of circumcision is to effect a qualitative change. He or she is a whole new person. Absent initiation, the man remains a boy, the woman a girl.

Conclusion

Foremost in the African library is the autobiography of God, who is known and experienced in the universe. God, who is creator and sustainer, and father-mother, is an experienced, intimate facet of daily life. The descendants of *Mwambu* and *Sela* discover and express their religious consciousness and spirituality in their culture, their language, rites of initiation, the veneration of their ancestors, and their belief in the world of spirits. All things exist for the welfare of humanity. These are the foundations of African Traditional Religions.

The Eye of God

CHAPTER II

More of the Lion's Tale ...
Christianity in Africa

Early History

Since its foundation, Christianity has existed in Africa, but it is not the first imported religion to have followers on the continent; it was preceded by Judaism. The oldest Jewish community in Africa was made up of the *Falasha* Jews, who formed part of the *Agao* people of Ethiopia, a culture dating back more than two thousand years. They consider themselves to be of the tribe of Dan, and the indigenous representatives of Judaism in Africa.

Christianity first found its way to Africa shortly after its inception in what is today known as Palestine. It has persisted in Egypt and Ethiopia ever since, despite being eliminated in most other areas of North Africa and eastern Sudan, particularly during the early years of Islamic expansion under the Umayyad dynasty, which lasted from 661-750 C.E.

Early African Christianity was torn by controversy, including dissonance regarding the nature of Christ. African monks denied the missionaries' claim that Christ had two natures, divine and human, instead contending that Christ had only one divine nature, which philosophy led to the term *monophysite*, literally meaning "one nature." This belief became the foundation of Coptic Christianity, which endures today in Egypt, Ethiopia, and the former kingdom of Nubia, where Christianity was translated into local languages.

For myriad reasons, the growth of the early North African church was greatly compromised. From its beginning, the church was established as metropolitan and Latin-speaking. It held in contempt the culture of the Berbers, a North African tribe now largely Arabized and Islamic. Membership comprised the social elite—the Latin speaking minority who had Latin names and were culturally Latinized, living and promoting the values of classical society. The indigenous poor were heavily taxed and exploited.

The Second Phase of Evangelization

The fifteenth and sixteenth centuries inaugurated a second phase of Christian evangelization in Africa, this phase focused bi-coastally, south of the Sahara, and was carried out largely by Portuguese missionaries whose King supported Portugal's commercial interests more than the spread of Christianity. African scholar and theologian John Mbiti points out that "the Missions became ecclesiastical colonies and the strong effort to root the faith in the African cultures and in the life of the people lacked commitment. Eventually, the Church became extinct here."[1]

Nineteenth century Africa arrived with Western missionaries proselytizing for quite a different Christianity from that of the early church. Fractured by the Protestant Reformation, influenced by capitalism, and conditioned to reflect European cultures and nationalism,[2] this modern Christianity was accompanied by sundry missionary societies, each of whom ascribed to different forms of worship and theology, belonged to different nation-states, and competed for influence among the African peoples. Believing in the superiority of their cultures, missionaries promoted European, Western, Roman, and Latinized cultures as the only tool with which to Christianize the African people. Such triumphal arrogance did nothing to enhance the African people's trust and confidence. In the African's judgment,

Europe was prepared to offer its religion, language and culture to Africans, but only in exchange for the land, mines, labor, energy and other economic riches of Africa. Jomo Kenyatta, the first president of the Republic of Kenya was more prescient than even he may have realized when he observed: "When the white man came to Africa he had the Bible and we had the land. And now we have the Bible and he has the land."[3]

The Third Phase of Evangelization

Two German missionaries, John Rebman and Richard Kraph, ushered in a third era of Christian evangelization, opening their first church in East Africa in 1846 at Rabai, near Mombasa, Kenya. Though they learned to speak the local language and invited the people to church services, they exemplified the cultural insensitivity of their evangelistic predecessors. A few people attended their service, and when it was finished, the missionaries rushed to the entrance of the building to hear the people's reactions—they were far from enthusiastic. Asked whether they would come again the following Sunday, the people's firm answer was "No." Asked why, they answered that they were accustomed to worshipping in another way. An animal should have been slaughtered, they said, and there should have been food and plenty to drink. There should have been drumming, singing, and dancing. Rebmann and Kraph informed the people that their reaction revealed them to be sinners. They explained the Christian doctrine of sin and sinners, and the local people felt slandered. The missionaries replied that "God had sent his only Son so that they might know that God loved them. Surely, they could understand this love because God had given them life, children, the sun and the moon, the rain and the harvest, their clothing and their beer."[4]

Though well meaning, Rebman and Kraph expressed the chronic condition of hopeful missionaries: want of cultural sensitivity. Lacking humility and a cross-cultural understanding of their position, they failed to ask and learn the value of the Kenyans' extant religious practices; instead, they passed judgment. Evangelicals, local or missionary, are tasked to learn, listen, observe and search for meaning. They must avoid passing judgment on a culture, or aspects of it, and try to grasp its authenticity.

When Pope John Paul II visited Africa in 1985, one hundred and fifty years after the first missionaries, he had a different experience. During the celebration of Mass at Uhuru Park, Nairobi, live animals, fruits, beer and sugar cane were brought to the altar as offerings. Two goats, tied to the altar, bleated throughout the Mass! Drums were played and people danced with joy.

The Blossoming of African Christianity

African Christianity expanded rapidly in the first half of the 20th century, through the joint efforts of overseas missionaries and African converts. Mission schools became nurseries of Christian congregations, and many converts earned the name of catechist, or reader.[5] Personal, free choice occasioned religious conversions; however, the societal and economic benefits of conversion offered a powerful incentive.

Christian-sponsored education played a significant role in the process of Christian conversion in Africa. The acquisition of a Western style education became the *sine qua non* for personal betterment in terms of enabling young men to find employment as clerks, engineers and teachers, as well as providing the means to fight colonialism. Most African religious teachers and evangelists were not formally educated. Still today, most chiefs and headmen do not become Christians, but they do encourage the tribe and their own children to be converted.

Today, sects and denominations from Europe and America are perceived as competitors; as a result, African people have no single image of Christianity, but variations on a theme. As African theologian John Mbiti points out this has led each denomination to promote its own version of the Christian message. African people are experiencing a multiplicity of imported church structures and traditions with little cultural adaptation. The typical African Christian can not appreciate the differences between what are often conflicting forms of Christianity. These denominations endeavor far more to produce perfect Anglicans, perfect Roman Catholics, perfect Lutherans, perfect Baptists or Quakers than to make converts into good followers of Jesus Christ.

The current increasing rate of Christian conversion in Africa is one of the most astonishing religious phenomena of our time. According to Archbishop Gabriel Gonsum Ganaka of Jos, Nigeria, the Catholic population of Africa has steadily increased since 1927. The following statistics were presented at the African Synod held in Rome April 1994: in 1927, there were 3.2 million Catholics in Africa; by 1993, there were 95 million. In 1939 there were only 2 bishops in Africa, and by 1993 there were 327 bishops, while the number of diocesan priests increased from 127 in 1927 to 10,903 in 1993.

Walbert Buhlmann, a professor at the Gregorian University in Rome, acknowledges this tremendous activity, stating:

It is no exaggeration to say that so great success in so short a time has never been recorded in the history of the missions. Africa, last of the continents, has suddenly overtaken the others and won the prize. These singing and dancing people... must have something to offer the church and mankind.[6]

However, as Bishop Sarpong of Ghana recently warned:

The church appears to be gaining a foothold in Africa. The increase of the number of Christians over the past years has been phenomenal. On Sundays our churches are packed. Extra church activities, choirs, scripture unions, Legion of Mary, Knights are seen everywhere. But I think it would be a sad mistake for us to be complacent. All these seem to me to be superficial. In fact, Christianity and Christian conviction are only skin deep.[7]

A Zairean song commonly heard in Kenya expresses it in this way:

Miserable Christian
At Mass in the morning
To the fortune teller in the evening
The amulet in the pocket
The scapular around the neck.[8]

Concerned, knowledgeable observers are describing the syncretism of African tribal religions and Christianity, arguing that deeply rooted tribal customs and traditions persist, while Christianity is lived out on a superficial level. Baptism may incorporate the African into the family of God, but tribal relationships take precedence. Blood is thicker than water.

Understanding the rapid growth of African Christianity promises to be valuable, and may benefit the Western church, currently beset by rapid decline and crises. A Kikuyu proverb states: *A river is enlarged by its tributaries.* Consider, then, that African traditions and cultures constitute some of the many tributaries that enlarge this human river. African spiritual values hold tremendous potential to positively influence those who seek to understand them, and may serve to call people back to their roots and give them new meaning and purpose in life. The African experience speaks proudly to critical spiritual issues, such as the meaning of life, suffering, peace, and human relationships. These singing and dancing people do indeed have something to offer the church and mankind.

The poetic and mystical Jesuit scholar Pierre Teilhard de Chardin would have delighted in this development of Christianity in Africa:

> He was convinced that the first human home was in Africa. This conjure is supported by the recent discoveries by the Leakey family on the shores of Lake Turkana in Kenya. There in East Africa, the Leakeys reveal, humankind formed its first culture in relation to surrounding nature. There in East Africa, humanity thought out its first theologies and its first survival patterns. According to Teilhard, humanity went out from there to spread over the earth, adapting and developing over millions of years to all kinds of environments. Now, after having wondered all over the globe, those emigrants are returning to their original home, to their own roots, to their sources, to the fountain of human life.[9]

The first Christian missionaries to Africa in modern times did not think in Teilhard's terms. They came to convert; they came to save, to win souls. What a paradox it would be if Divine Providence has us as witness to the African Christian church converting the universal church, saving the saviors, winning the soul of the Western church.

Conclusion

In its first century in existence, Christianity arrived in Africa, first in Ethiopia and then across North Africa. Christianity's lack of success in North Africa was largely the result of its failure to indigenize or contextualize itself with African culture, and also due to the expansion of Islam (to be discussed in the following chapter). Today, Christianity persists only as a minority religion in this region, represented largely by Coptic Christianity.

A second era of evangelical Christianity in Africa occurred between the fifteenth and sixteenth centuries, south of the Sahara. Christianity was asserted into the contexts of Western economic and political colonialism, along the sectarian divisions of the European Protestant Reformation, factors which substantially weakened the Christian message.

Burgeoning missionary Christianity was not prepared for serious encounters with either the traditional religions or the modern cultural and technological changes taking place in Africa. Even so, the Christian church is flourishing in its third historical period of expansion in Africa, begun in the mid-nineteenth century. Its notable success has been somewhat compromised by continuing debate concerning inculturation, or the contextualization of Christianity and African Traditional Religions.

Allah

CHAPTER III

The Lion Continues to Roar ...
Islam in Africa

The emphasis to this point has been African Traditional Religions and Christianity. Of concern now is Islam, a religion deeply rooted in the African continent. Like Christianity, Islam is making a claim on the African people, particularly in those areas where African Traditional Religions are dominant. Because Arabic is the chief language of Islam and the transmitter of Arab culture, this component of The Lion's Tale will illuminate how the Arabic language influences African cultural languages, especially that of the *Bantu* peoples.

At this juncture, it is important to clearly define what is meant by the word Islam. Islam is the name of the religion as stated in the Holy Qur'an; its adherents are Muslims. In its broader meaning, every object in the universe is Islamic to Muslims in the sense that the universe is submissive to the will of Allah. The Qur'an says, "This day I have perfected you, your religion and completed my favor on you, and chosen for you Islam as a religion" (Qur'an 5:3). "Surely, the true religion with Allah is Islam" (Qur'an 3:18).

The two foundational stones of Islam are the Qur'an, along with the Sunna and the Hadith. These constitute the primary source of *Shari'ah* law.

The Qur'an is Islam's holy book, believed to be the message of Allah as transmitted by the Angel Gabriel, in Arabic, to the Prophet Muhammad. The Sunna and the Hadith are a record of the life of the Prophet; his deeds and sayings, respectively. Shari'ah law is Allah's law, and the Muslim's guide to living a virtuous life.

A worldwide faith, Islam is regionally varied and even community-specific. Outside of North Africa, Islam assimilated, or contextualized, the cultures of African people. African Islam can be appreciated only by first understanding the beliefs and practices of Islam as enunciated in the Qur'an, the Sunna and the Hadith.

The Growth of Islam in Africa

Africa holds a special place in global Islamic history. It is second only to Asia in its number of Muslims. Ethiopia served as a place of refuge for the first Muslims who were persecuted in the time of the Prophet Muhammad. Egypt was under Islamic rule ten years after the Prophet's death 632 C.E., and all the southern shores of the Mediterranean were occupied by the year 700 C.E. During that time, Islam was mainly based in northern, urban areas. Sub-Saharan Africa offered relatively few towns and cities. In such rural areas, as among the *Bantu* speaking peoples and *Nilotic* tribes, Islam found it difficult to establish itself.

The expansion of Islam in Africa followed three routes. Accomplished via Arab military conquest, Islam moved firstly through Egypt, continuing west through the Sahara, and then towards the south and west. Islamic expansion then linked the ports of southern Arabia with the coast of east Africa on the Indian Ocean. Finally, there was a move through Somalia and northern Ethiopia.

Initially, unlike North Africa, sub-Saharan African Islam was not spread by military action, but by trade, including slave trade, which remains of ambiguous impact. Military occupation never played a significant role in the historical process of Islamizing eastern Africa. Islam arrived in the seventh century on the east coast of Africa, where Arab settlements were already established and growing, thanks to flourishing trade. On the Indian Ocean, Islam has deep roots, especially centered in Zanzibar, Mombasa, Lamu, Malindi, Kilwa, Mogadishu and many other cities and islands along the east coast of Africa.

The greatest increase of Muslims south of the Sahara occurred recently, during the colonial era. In eastern and western Africa, the growth of Islam was a reaction to European colonial domination, backed by the leaders of the *Sufi* brotherhood. These were militant Islamic groups that sought to revitalize Islam through internal reform, thus enabling Islamic societies to resist foreign control. Saudi Arabia, Egypt, Sudan and Libya were at the forefront of this militant reform movement in Islam.

Divisions in African Islam

Islam is fractured, though its fragmentation is unimpressive in comparison to the various denominations and sects of Christianity. Although most Islamic sects originated outside Africa, they have African characteristics. For example, the dynamic *Ahmadiyya* sect was founded in the nineteenth century by Ghulan Ahmad, a native of India. Its goal is the reformation of Islamic orthodoxy. Many are converts from African Christianity. It is very active and growing in Africa.

The *Shi'ite* sect is represented chiefly on the east coast of Africa, mainly among immigrant Muslims of Indo-Pakistani origin. The Shi'ites invest both religious guidance and political leadership in the *imam,* who is related by blood to Muhammad. The Shi'ites believe in continuous divine guidance through a divinely inspired guide, the imam, who is the final authoritative interpreter of Allah's will as expressed in the Qur'an and the Sunnah of the Prophet.

Among the *Sunni,* only religious, not political direction is entrusted to the *caliph,* who is elected by the collective judgment of the community (*ijma*). The caliph is the selected successor of the Prophet, who succeeds to spiritual leadership, but not to the Prophet Muhammad's political authority. "After the death of Muhammad, Sunni Islam came to place the final religious authority in interpreting Islam in the consensus (*ijma*) or collective judgment of the community."[1] Those who are not learned in the law do not participate in the selection of the caliph.

What distinguishes Sunnis and Shi'ites is not that one is conservative and one liberal, or differences in each sect's interpretation of Shari'ah. The same in fundamental Islamic beliefs and practices, they are nourished by the same sources of the Qur'an, the Sunnah, and the Hadith. The crucial difference lies only in the matter of leadership. Thus, the fundamental difference between Sunni and Shi'ite Muslims is the Shi'ite doctrine of the *Imamate* as distinct from the Sunni *Caliphate.*"[2]

The *Ismaelis* constitute the rather militant wing of the Shi'ite sect, and boast few African converts. This sect, though small in number, is financially powerful under the direction of its wealthy leader, His Highness, the Aga Khan, and very politically active, particularly so with regard to social services, especially education and medicine. Their social services are available to everyone.

Swahili People and Islam

Kiswahili is one of the most commonly spoken languages in Africa. The word *Swahili* comes from an Arabic word which means "coast," and first referred to the *Bantu* people living along the east coast of the Indian Ocean, whose language derived from a combination of Arabic and older Bantu languages. Islam is often used to identify Swahili culture; Swahili and Islam are synonymous along the east coast of Africa. However, some indigenous Africans describe themselves as *Waswahili*, wishing to establish themselves as an autonomous tribal entity, distinct from other Africans. For example, the distinctive costume of the (*Swahili*) man is the *kanzu,* a long skirt, and the *kofia*, an embroidered cap. However, times are changing. Since political independence in the 1960s, it is difficult to distinguish the Waswahili as a separate people.

Language and Culture

The impact of the Arabic language in sub-Saharan Africa cannot be underestimated. It is a medium of worship, of commerce, and for indigenous African languages, a source of loan words. This is particularly true of such languages as *Hausa* and *Wolof* (West Africa), *Kiswahili,* and *Somali* (East Africa). Some of these deeply Arabic-based indigenous languages have in turn influenced neighboring languages. For the sake of clarity, here are some examples: The Swahili word *jamaa* is commonly used among the peoples of east Africa to refer to community or family, and is derived from the Arabic word *jama'a*, which means a custom that is recognized by the majority of the people in a given place and time. As another example, the Arabic word is *ayb*, means shame. In *Kiswahili, aibu* carries the same meaning. There is a Swahili proverb which is: *Aibu ya maiti ajua mwosha*, meaning, "The corpse washer knows the defects of the deceased." The Muslims have their dead washed before burial. The corpse washer is the only person likely to ever know the physical defects of the dead.

Kiswahili: A Cultural Impact

The fusion of various Islamic elements and the *Bantu* languages led to the present day Swahili cultural synthesis. Swahili culture is a composite of African tribal religions and Islam. By direct product of African people's assimilation of the Arabic language with their own, Islam found success where Christianity did not: Islam was contextualized.

About a thousand years ago, on the east coast of Africa, Kenyan and Tanzanian peoples developed what was destined to be black Africa's most successful indigenous language, *Kiswahili*. This language is now also widely spoken in Uganda, Zaire, Rwanda and Burundi, Mozambique and Malawi as well. It is being taught in select universities in other parts of Africa, Europe, the United States, Russia and some parts of Asia. Of all the African languages used in international commerce and electronic communication, Kiswahili is the most common, as it is used from Beijing to London, from Bombay to Washington, D.C.

The east African coast is also the cradle of much classical Swahili poetry and music, a frequent function of which is the expression of stressful emotions related to personal, social, or cultural conflicts. Some of the oldest masterpieces of Swahili poetry came from such ancient Swahili cities as Lamu, Pate, and Mvita (now Mombasa), Muyaka, Utenzi wa Mwana Kupona, and Inkishafi.

Conclusion

Islam established itself by military conquest in northern Africa in the mid-seventh century C.E. The indigenous population was completely refashioned; that is, the Arabic language and culture, as well as

Islamic religion, displaced not only the traditional African religions, languages and cultures, but also nascent Christianity.

In later centuries, Islam was propagated in sub-Saharan Africa by commerce and trade, including slave trade. In more modern times, Islam gained strength by allying itself with the anti-colonial spirit of the African peoples. Through its language, Islam was contextualized with African Traditional Religions and cultures, and thus perceived by African peoples as offering more than European colonial Christianity and culture. The next chapter of the Lion's Tale will discuss in greater detail the modern impact of Islam in Africa.

CHAPTER IV

The Lion is Angry...
Major African Religous and Cultural Conflicts

The African continent is in the throes of what is being described as a struggle for "second independence"; that is, for political democratization analogous to its struggle in the 1960s for independence from colonial and political domination. The continent is burdened with economic decline and indebtedness, tragic suffering compounded by the economic policies of multinational corporations such as the International Monetary Fund (IMF), the World Bank, and the World Trade Organization (WTO). As never before, Africans are buffeted by forces competing for their souls, their allegiance, and their abundant natural resources. Prior allegiances are dying. New ones are being formed.

The Current Situation

Major forces of conflict and change in Africa today include African Traditional Religions, Christianity, Islam and secularism. In this conflict lie abundant opportunities for the enrichment of Africa, as well, perhaps, as for a transformation of Western secularism and the forces of modernity, some of which are more detrimental than beneficial to Africans. These opportunities are not without their attendant risks to African people, but it may be argued that through a process of authentic dialogue between its competing forces, African peoples might be enriched, and emerge from conflict more beautiful. *Negra est pulchra*: black is beautiful. And the beautification of Africa means the beautification of the world.

Western Secularism and De-Africanization

"The ancestors of Africa are angry,"[1] says Ali Mazrui a world-renowned academic and political writer on African and Islamic studies. For those who believe in the power of their ancestors, evidence of this anger is visible everywhere: revolution, genocide, famine, disease, colonization, poverty, dislocation, ethnic clashes, and millions of refugees. This is the reality of modern Africa. Such discordance is perceived by Africans as the failing attempt of secular forces to modernize Africa without reciprocated cultural interaction with the African peoples. African history and values often appear to be largely irrelevant.

The changes that have come with westernization and urbanization are seducing Africans to forget the values and cultures of their ancestors. A deep chasm between a people and their cultures is forming. This is the process of disconnecting Africa from the African. Traditional life is undermined, such that tribal identity is fading away. Other values are making claims on the individual and the community. Materialism dictates tastes and desires, values and dreams. The élan of secularism seduces African people to use what they do not invent and purchase what they cannot repair.

In an earlier time, American slave owners attempted to force the stolen children of Africa to abandon their culture, using the slogan: "Forget you are African, but remember you are black." Africa's modern children are being confronted with the cruel, false, seductive mandate, "Forget you are African."[2]

The enormous influence of secularism abounds in modern Africa's lifestyles, largely in evidence of exported Western popular culture. Clothing, music, housing, cars, communication technologies, sports equipment, and even food preferences have been imported, along with its moral values and behavior. The possession of first world goods carries with it great social value. Many people of poor financial means are willing to spend great sums for products which carry the label "made in America" (or Japan or England). Many Western products are acquired more quickly than the technological skills needed to maintain or repair them, as is often seen in the African transport systems: autos, trucks and buses languish by the roadside, broken-down because parts and repair skills are lacking. Such tribulations are often exacerbated by foreign exchange problems engineered by the World Bank, the IMF, and the WTO.

Further evidence of Western-exported secularism in Africa is reflected in the proliferation of foreign languages, including English, French, German, Portuguese, Japanese, and Chinese. Those who speak foreign languages have higher social status and are preferred choices for leadership positions in government. Thus, traditional African languages experience significant decline. A people who have been linguistically conquered rarely require the threat of arms to be kept in control.

The English poet Alexander Pope wrote that, "Western modernity is a dangerous thing, drink deep or taste not western springs." In other words, newly freed from direct foreign government control, Africans remain dependent on foreign handouts, foreign financing, and foreign investment. Africa's ability to produce by and for itself has been severely impaired.

Julius Nyerere, the founder of the Republic of Tanzania, once reflected:

> While the great powers are trying to get to the moon, we are trying to get to the village. Well, the great powers have been to the moon and back, and are now even communicating with the stars. But in Africa, we are still trying to reach the village. What's more, the village is getting even more remote with worsening communications even further into the distance.[3]

The financial and human cost of the adoption of Western consumer culture has become a great hardship for Africa. Truly, Africa is at war. This is a war of cultures, between indigenous, ancestral Africa and the forces of modern civilization. Nyerere reminded his countrymen that they were the custodians of the soil of their ancestors and trustees of their descendants. They had no right to hand over to their children soil that was less fertile than what they inherited from their forefathers. Whether Africans will heed this message of trusteeship remains to be seen.

New Contending Forces Seeking the Soul of Africa

Besides secularism, Christianity and Islam continue competing for the soul of Africa, the outcome of which struggle for souls is dubious. Startling statements and claims are bandied about, such as that "five times as many people are becoming Muslims in Africa as are becoming Christians."[4] Many question which religion will dominate sub-Saharan Africa. More than forty years ago, Anglican Bishop, missionary and author S.C. Neill, wrote that five forces were contending for the African soul. According to Neil, the five forces were old African traditions, Islam, Christianity, sheer materialism, and communism.[5] Neil noted that it was not yet clear in whose hands the future of sub-Saharan Africa would belong. North of the Sahara, Africa is almost one hundred percent Islamic. Communism is no longer a threat, having been overpowered by religious and political forces. And so the question remains, what is next for Africa?

The Crusading Approach of Islam

For a multiplicity of African people around the continent, the crusading expansion of Islam seems to be the answer. Islam has a strong, growing appeal based on its success in counteracting secularism and economic domination. Islam exhibits strong infusive potential, presenting itself as an African religion and making fewer demands on native peoples to change than does Christianity. Nevertheless, it quickly refashions the life of an entire tribe. This process is sometimes described as Arabization and/or Islamization.

The expansion of Islam in the seventh century C.E. was much faster than that of any other world religion. Unlike Christianity and Buddhism, two other major world religions, Islam has remained successful in its geographical origin, Saudi Arabia. The Arabs are the most successful exporters of their own religion in human history. By way of contrast, Europeans and Americans have exported a borrowed religion, Christianity.

Muslims, wherever they are, form one nation. It is religious faith which decides nationality in Islam, and not the geographical territory, color, race, or language of its adherents. And Islam is rapidly increasing as a worldwide religion. Demographic studies indicate that the number of Muslims is multiplying both by natural increase (most Muslims rejoice in numerous children, and Islam officially prohibits birth control), and by conversion.

The New Islamic Consciousness

Two sources of Islamic adaptation across Africa have been set in motion: Arabization, through imposition of Arab language and lifestyle, and Islamization, or religious conversion. Through the use of local and national mass media, as well as by a flood of Islamic publications and video cassettes, the culture and values of Islamic life are now transmitted to even the most remote African villages in local, tribal languages.

It can be misleading to speak in general terms about African Islam. Where Islam accesses areas dominated by traditional religions, it is deeply colored by local tribal customs, establishing quasi-customized types of Islam in various countries. In order to survive in these areas, Islam accepts and assimilates existing African culture; thus, it is contextualized. For the African, the tribe is the medium in which religion takes shape and is experienced. It is in tribal life that the meaning of myths expressing who a people are, where they come from, and where they are going, is communicated. Myth is the seat of a people's worldview. Islam contextualizes itself in tribal mythology.

Islamic cultural history reveals that its strength has always been its urban stronghold. The Prophet Muhammad himself found support for his new religion among the scattered rural tribes of Arabia; however, it was among his urban kinsmen, the tribe of *Quraysh* in Mecca and Medina, that Islam was established and where it gained momentum for expansion. Islam still experiences difficulties in establishing itself in rural villages. In the cities and towns, with their great influx of Muslims, the rapid expansion and growing influence of Islam is most evident. Muslims can be found running small businesses at trading centers and markets along the highways. Mosques are multiplying in urban centers.

In rural Africa, residents often perceive Islam as a disintegrative factor. From the rural perspective, Islam is viewed much the same as mainline Christianity; that is, to be just another divisive influence on local culture. On the other hand, in the towns, where life and personal relationships are more secularized, Islam is viewed as an integrative factor. City life and commerce often result in the abandonment of local African Traditional Religions. Islam is experienced as a constructive, community-building force. The public call to prayer on Friday is a unifying experience for the *umma* (community).

In sub-Saharan African cities where Islam is flourishing, trade serves as the backbone of the local economy. Both wholesale trade and commerce and the street sales are mainly run by Muslims. Restaurants (*mikahawa*), which in Africa are termed hotels, are generally controlled by Muslims. Heavy commercial transportation trucks are manned by Muslims; fleets of trucks transporting gasoline from the coastal city of Mombasa in Kenya, and traveling to Uganda, Tanzania, Rwanda/Burundi, DRC (Democratic Republic of Congo), and southern Sudan on their return, are heave with timber and food, especially bananas, to be sold in the major cities along the highways.

The migration of young people from tribal areas of sub-Saharan Africa into the cities looking for job opportunities is likewise a great boon to Islam. Upon arrival in the cities, these young people find themselves completely cut off from their families and tribal ties. While looking for employment in the cities, they are often housed and fed by Muslim communities. In a short time, tribal religions and cultures are abandoned and Islam is chosen to fill the vacuum created by the loss of traditional society and mores.

A Special Case: The Islamization of Sudan

One of the countries in Africa that is most violently caught up in a whirlwind of change is Sudan. In the Darfur region of western Sudan, the citizens are black Muslims. The Sudanese government, using Arab "*Janjaweed*" militias, its air force, and organized starvation are systematically killing the black Sudanese Muslims of Darfur in an attempt to impose Arab culture and claim their land.

In southern Sudan, the Islamic government is forcefully attempting to instill Arab culture and Islamic practices in the Christians and traditional believers. This African-Arab conflict along the Nile Valley requires a careful study. In essence, it is a conflict of autonomy, with one foot rooted in "Africanism" and another in "Arabism." But it is not merely a subject of ethnicity. The northern Sudanese perceive themselves as Arabs, and whether their Arabness is more by acquisition than heredity is of little importance. On the other hand, the southern Sudanese see themselves as legitimate, non-Arab Africans.

As is the case in so many former colonial states in Africa, the geographical structuring of Sudan upon the departure of the British in 1956 continues to generate warfare to this very day:

> The imperial regime decided to keep the south as a human zoo and to concentrate economic and educational development in the north. Subsequently, British interests dictated on the eve of imperial withdrawal that the two regions should be united administratively and that political power should be handed to the Arabs.[6]

Southern Sudan was deliberately excluded from the constitutional negotiation table. Southern Sudanese resorted to violence to protest the change of colonial rule from the British to the Arabs. This is the situation in which Sudan finds itself today. Under president Ja'afar Nimeri, Sudan introduced Islamic law, or Shari'ah law. And so in practice, under the Sudanese military regime, Islamic moral law and civil law are one in southern Sudan. Those acts which Shari'ah determines to be wrong or immoral are punishable in the court of law. For example, robbers and thieves, under some conditions, might have their offending hand amputated. Or, under Sharia'h law, a Muslim who converts to another religion could be sentenced to death. The punishment for apostasy is death and any Muslim who advocates apostasy or declares apostasy openly by word or through an act, and who refuses to relent, having been given time allowed by the court for repentance, will be sentenced to death.

Shari'ah law is the sum total of the Muslim way of life. It is the path leading to peace and submission to the will of Allah. Shari'ah law is the Qur'an, the Sunnah and Hadith of the Prophet. Therefore, Shari'ah law is the heart of Islam, and strict obedience to Shari'ah is the core of Islam. In the general context, then, all Muslims adhere to Shari'ah law, the universally defining Islamic constitution; however, it is important to note that Shari'ah law can and does include local distinction, dependent on the interpretation of and additions to Shari'ah by local Islamic governance. It is at this point, the point of political interpretation, that Shari'ah results in Islamic cultural differences between, for example, Northern Nigeria and Libya, Iran and Bangladesh.

Traditional Religions and Islam

As discussed in chapter one, African Traditional Religions must be understood in light of the adherent's special respect for his ancestors. Veneration of the ancestors becomes a source of conflict when Islam encounters African Traditional Religions. Usually, the thinking and customs of African people with regard to their ancestors will prevail when encountering Islam. For an African, the universal, all-powerful God, though real and ever present, is not experienced as close to humans as are the spirits of the living dead and the ancestors. Such religious thinking and experience in regard to ancestral veneration is the occasion of theological dispute with Islam. The issue of religious tolerance is a challenge to Islam, which officially allows no compromise with the unity of Allah or with submission to Allah's will. Mediation or compromise is officially not permitted in Islam. The Muslim conscience is troubled by African ancestral veneration, which is perceived as worshipping false gods. But in practice, Islam lives alongside the ancestors. African Traditional Religions accommodate Islam, and Islam must accommodate African Tradition Religions. In some cases, ancestor veneration dies a slow death, its passing not seeming to be harmful to the African people. Western secularism and Islam are but two of the forces contending for the soul of Africa. The third force is Christianity.

African Christianity

Most of today's African churches developed during the colonial period, from 1880 to 1960. This period introduced many modern infrastructures such as Christian schools and social services which facilitated the work of evangelization. But the European missionaries did not understand at that time how much Africa had suffered politically and economically from colonialism, which subjugated the entire continent into subservience. As the anti-colonial spirit increased, the subjugated Africans feared the approaching moment of independence: would Christianity be swept away with colonialism?

Today, forty years after Africa secured its independence from European invasion, two facts stand out. First, today's African Christians are able to distinguish the essence of Christianity from its European trappings. Those who have discarded both and have embraced Islam, or who have gone back to the religion of their ancestors are a small minority. It is an unquestionable fact that statistically, since 1990, Christianity has become the most widespread religion in sub-Saharan Africa. African Christianity is stabilized and strong. The second fact is that despite consolidation, Christianity in Africa has serious problems. One problem is the infiltration of secularism, especially evident in growing cities.

Yet another problem is the divisiveness of the various Christian denominations, inherited from the mother churches. More than on any other continent, this ecclesiastical fragmentation continues and is fed by the constant influx of new foreign-based Christian sects and the tendency of African people to live, worship, and serve one another in small communities. This enduring church division problem is especially apparent in the Christian African Independent/Indigenous Churches (AICs).

The attraction that these groups hold for even the educated population relates to a third problem, which is inculturation. Even though many African Christians are comfortable with the European aspects of their church and consider them integral parts of traditional Christianity, a growing number of the faithful feel the need for a deeper contextualization of their Christian faith with their African cultures. The majority of church leaders understand the necessity of inculturation, but not its urgency. Only a minority of leaders are seeking solutions that go beyond the introduction of local songs in the liturgy.

Many Christian scholars are of the opinion that the Achilles' heel of Christian evangelizing is the official church's resistance to inculturation or contextualization of the Gospel, not only in Africa but also in other parts of the world. The desire to root the Gospel in local realities is becoming a fundamental option demanded by the proclamation of the Good News.

Christianity, when understood as Gospel or Good News, is not just an ideology or theology, but is a way of life. The Good News is neither a macro-economic theory nor a set of Marxian theses and antitheses. It is not an exercise in logic. It contains the Good News of God's message of love, exemplified by Christ. Thus, when realized in a particular day and time, it has the potential to enrich all cultures, ideologies, and social structures. The Good News is catholic, meaning universal. It can purify and enrich all, in the fashion of salt and light and fire. Therefore, Africans do not have to choose between being Christian and being African. They can be both Christian and African. African Traditional Religions and Christianity can complement each other.

The term culture, in its general usage, includes the totality of a people's way of life. Christianity is not to be identified exclusively with a particular culture, language, or political/economic organization of people or nations. Becoming a Christian demands not acceptance of Western culture; rather, conversion to the Christian does demand that the convert takes on Christ as the ideal. Christian conversion should help a person to challenge and to enrich his own culture. The Christian is to communicate his faith, the Good News, chiefly by the example of his life of caring, sharing, creative love. His love can be expressed and communicated authentically through the use of cultural media; for example, art, music, dance, story telling, and traditional ritual ceremonies and celebrations.

Historical experience demonstrates that Christian evangelical efforts in Africa have often failed or been gravely impeded by the refusal of their proponents to respect and incorporate local cultural values and practices into its evangelical efforts. Reflecting that truth, another weakness of Christian missionary efforts has been its insistence on imposing a Western Christian culture on African peoples. For example, in September 1923, a document was issued in Stanleyville, now Kisangani, Democratic Republic of Congo, by the Roman Catholic bishops and the Belgian Congo colonial government. The document described traditional customs that were considered harmful to public order. With stern words and warning, it forbade:

Offerings to spirits and ancestors; cooperation in ancestor rituals; dancing and hunting ceremonies; magical or religious rites on the occasion of a birth, or appearance of the children's teeth, or circumcision, or a girl's puberty, or marriage, or illness. Likewise forbidden were traditional rites in honor of the ancestors performed before hunting or fishing expeditions or carvings representing the spirits of the dead.[7]

Converts were expected to turn their backs on their traditional customs and way of life. Only then would it be considered that the Christian faith had indeed taken root in their hearts. Contradicting that, a positive message was issued to the African people by Pope Paul VI when he visited Kampala in 1969: "You may, and you must, have an African Christianity."[8] The Pope charged the African bishops to accept a different view of the role of culture. He encouraged adoption of local cultural values, saying:

> The split between the Gospel and the culture is without a doubt the drama of our time…Therefore, every effort must be made to ensure a full evangelization of culture, or more correctly of cultures. They have to be regenerated by an encounter with the Gospel.[9]

Pope Paul VI determination was that the Christian Gospel not only should enrich the culture in which it is proclaimed, but is also to be enriched by that culture; furthermore, that the dedicated, effective Christian missionary must be open to change and enrichment by encounter with African peoples. Successful Christian evangelization demands nothing less.

Jesus Christ taught his disciples that an inauthentic Gospel would not ring true; though a statistical giant, Christianity would be an anachronism. "You are like salt for the whole human race. But if salt loses its saltiness … it has become worthless, so it is thrown out (Matthew 5:13)."

Saint Paul echoes those Gospel words:

> Although I am not bound to anyone, I made myself the slave of all, so as to win over as many as possible. I became like a Jew to the Jews in order to win the Jews. To those bound by

the law, I became like one who is bound (although I am not bound by it), that I might win those bound by the law…To the weak I became weak with a view to winning the weak (1 Corinthians 9: 19-23).

Jesus mingled with the society of his earthly time, and by so doing made a profound impact on its members and its culture. If the church refuses to be influenced by and incorporated into the world in which it lives, then it will be like salt which has lost its taste.

Stop Gap Measures and Cultural Conflict

African Christians inherited a split persona. On one hand, they have accepted the norms imposed by foreign missionaries who discounted the values of African culture and exaggerated the values of Western culture. On the other hand, the African Christian cannot deny his own identity and cultural roots. As a result, the African Christian experiences a spiritual conflict of loyalties—a religious tug of war. Many seek to ameliorate this conflict by creating substitute religious practices and church communities, but too often the substitutes fail, resulting in more community dissension. There is an African saying in Kiswahili, *Jino la pembe si dawa ya pengo,* or, "An ivory tooth is not a cure for a gap." In other words, a substitute, however impressive, is never the real thing. As long as the gap exists between Christianity and African cultures, people will push to find a surrogate which, like the ivory tooth, may be attractive, but will never suffice.

Leadership and Inculturation

Bearing witness to the Christian message of peace and reconciliation is a major challenge for Africa's religious leaders. Recognized as servants of God, they enjoy great respect, but bishops, priests and those in religious or ministerial roles are challenged daily to earn the trust of the people. The religious leader must be perceived as a collaborator, in solidarity with the real living conditions of the people he serves. The Senegalese bishop Hyacinth Thiandoum, at the 1994 African Synod in Rome, wrote, "It would be a pity if a priest were to become part of the small cream of affluent elite in a sea of misery. He must avoid becoming just a maintenance man in an established church."[10]

A Christian leader serves all, regardless of creed, race, color or class. Ministerial success must not be measured merely by numbers of converts.

Jesus Christ commissioned his disciples not to win souls, but to make disciples of all nations, teaching them to observe all that he commanded (Matt. 28:19-20).

Christianity: Conflict with African Traditions

Lobengula, King of Ndebele, like many other Africans, believed that God had given to each people the culture he intended for them:

> ...he believed God had made all things as he wanted them. He had made all people and that he had made every country and tribe just as he wished them to remain; he believed God made the Amandebele as he wished them to be and it was wrong for anyone to seek to alter them.[11]

Lubengula attempted to correct missionary misunderstandings, telling them, "We do not believe that the killing of an ox or burning particular herbs makes rain, but these are the means by which we ask it, just as you ask it by reading your book and saying prayers."[12]

Early Christian missionaries came to Africa with distorted views about the lives of native people. They came ready to proselytize to the Africans, without asking the Africans to contribute. Jomo Kenyatta suggests that, as far as religion is concerned, the African was regarded as a clean slate on which anything could be written.[13] In the process of evangelization, there was to be no reciprocation between the senders and the recipients of the Christian message. Kenyatta further explains that the African was supposed to take wholeheartedly all religious dogmas of the white man and keep them sacred and unchanged, no matter how alien they were to the African way of life.[14] Africa has indeed paid heavily for this change which was initially forced upon her from the outside. In the final analysis, it is Africans who have experienced the change, and who must accept or reject it.

The Europeans were convinced that everything the African did or thought was evil, Kenyatta continues.[15] This belief resulted in mission failure. Instead of accepting the Gospel message, the African people turned a deaf ear to it. Kenyatta concludes that:

Missionaries endeavored to rescue the depraved souls of the African from the eternal fire; they set out to uproot the African, body and soul, from his own customs and beliefs, put him in a class by himself, with all his tribal conditions shattered and his institutions trampled upon.[16]

The Christian missionaries' thinking about African people was to a large extent shaped by horrific stories told them about African people for centuries. Writing in the sixteenth century, a Portuguese African explorer Duarte Lopez told of a great number of carved images of demons of varied and terrifying forms. Many people, he said, prayed to winged dragons; others have for their gods serpents, others rams, or tigers, or other horrible and loathsome beasts.[17] The Dutch historian Ofert Drapper in his book entitled, *A Comprehensive and Real Descriptive of Africa* published in 1668, filled his thick volume with observations which he summarized as follows: "The *Kaffir* (pagans) serve neither God nor idols. They know nothing at all about God but live like animals…People are lechers, thieves, swindlers, liars and gluttons and they are like animals rather than like men."[18]

Unsurprisingly, scholars and missionaries perceived Africans with a jaundiced eye. It is only today that this distorted perception is openly and clearly acknowledged by both the African people and foreign missionaries. Some angry Africans today argue that the Gospel has been betrayed by the church and its history of prejudice.

In its failure to inculturate itself in Africa, the Western Christian church failed to make the church a home for Africans. Home is where life starts, is nourished, and ends. A person's self-image, his dignity, his social status and his heart and soul are anchored in his home. "Home is where the heart is." But the European missionaries understood little. The bearers of Christ's message, in effect, attempted to destroy the cultural home of those they came to Christianize.

The Rise of Local Independent Christian Churches

The cultural insensitivity of foreign Christian missionaries has been counteracted by the many dissatisfied Christian converts inaugurating African Independent Christian Churches (AICs). AICs have proliferated, their members numbering now in the thousands. Many African Christians have abandoned Protestant and Catholic churches to become members of AICs. For example, in 1992, in Trans-kei, South Africa, one local Pentecostal church baptized *seventy thousand* converts in one day.[19] This proliferation of the AIC churches has led to the formation of new, locally based, but mainline Christian churches, such as the Church of Christ in Africa (CCA), an offshoot of the Anglican Church.

The African Israel Church-Nineveh (AICN), which evolved from Canadian Pentecostal missions, has responded to African traditions. Their founder's deference to the civil government and tribal cultures enabled the AICN to grow unopposed. For instance, polygamous men were admitted to church membership, but polygamy was denied for single or monogamous men after they joined the church. Women were afforded high status and leadership roles in this church, so that today, female membership outnumbers male by two to one.[20]

Another independent Christian denomination is the *Akorino* church, which started in the central province of Kenya among the Kikuyu people. The *Akorino* leaders do not allow their followers to go to a hospital when sick. Members are taught to depend entirely on God's healing power. Worshippers seek to be possessed by the spirit and to speak in tongues.

The Contemporary Status of African Independent Churches

To a great extent, the independent churches have become indigenous in leadership and organization, outside of missionary management. They are self-sufficient in many ways. They are not dependent on foreign aid; they have their own missionaries and church constitutions. Their missionary activity shows no sign of slowing down.

Another aspect of the AICs is that people tend to shop around for churches, changing religions as they would clothes. One missionary scholar likened the AIC movement to a jockey who rides a racing horse, as long as a horse is a fast runner. "When the horse loses its racing ability, the jockey chooses another horse, and by so doing, he remains on the race course."[21]

A large number of breakaway AIC churches are continuing to appear in western Kenya, Nigeria, and South Africa. This is a surprising development in an area like western Kenya, where the missionaries were so well received and the response to mission teaching so enthusiastic. What follows are some reasons for this AIC phenomenon.

Prior to the arrival of the missionaries, the *Luhyia* and *Luo* people had regular rhythms of worship. Ancestral veneration by means of prayer, medicine, offerings and sacrifices ensured successful harvest, sufficient rainfall, and protection from witchcraft. Anything that disturbed this traditional belief and practice was strongly challenged. The arrival of the Europeans and their wholly different culture initiated a crisis of untold damage: traditional ways were disturbed and people were troubled. The people began to be aware of a new threat to their traditional religion. Something had to be done to heal the wounds of this invasion, to reach rapprochement between the traditional and the new. The formation of local, fully acculturated, independent churches was the logical result.

Racial discrimination and land alienation also contributed to the rise of independent churches. Doubtlessly, this has heavily contributed to the tremendous proliferation of independent churches of both Ethiopian and Zionist character. Also, Kenya was beset for years by large numbers of white settlers. The colonial government was largely dominated by the interest of the settlers, in preference to the interests of the native population. This led Kenyans to suspect the motives of all white people and to no longer distinguish between the missionaries, the settlers, and the colonial administrators. A *Kikuyu* proverb summarizes this situation very well: "There is no difference between a Roman Catholic priest and a colonial settler: both are the same."

African Religious Separatism

Christianity first presented itself to Africa as divided among Lutherans, Anglicans, Roman Catholics, Greek Orthodox, and so forth. Amid the quotidian discord, the Africans naturally wondered why they shouldn't, as did the missionaries, have their own churches, founded and led independently. After all, homegrown products were often cheaper and better than imported ones. Politically, and in many other ways once led by the Europeans, there was now little incentive to concede to continuing religious subjugation.

Generally, the dynamic of missionary paternalism and domination explains why Africans continue to establish local, independent churches. Nationalist, anti-colonial and politically independent sentiment colludes to hasten and abet the AIC phenomenon. As long as the church remains predominantly in foreign hands, African people will rebel and find alternatives.

A further reason for the existence of AICs is described in the well-known East African phrase, "Christianity of the non-African is a Sunday morning faith," referring to the idea that people acknowledge God on Sunday, but live the remainder of the week without reference to God. However, for African people, living implies a continual chain of religiosity, from birth to death. For many Africans, this "Sunday morning faith" muffles the preaching of the Gospel. Also, Western missionary Christianity often seems more interested in building a church building than in building a church community, a phenomenon described by some as the "missionary edifice complex." Conversely, independent church communities are sanctuaries of creative fellowship, where Africans feel at home, share their needs and problems, shed their tears, rejoice in the Good News, help each other, and respond authentically to life.

Religion in traditional African society is found and experienced not on paper or in a building, but in people's hearts, minds, oral history, myths, rituals, and in their religious leaders (priests, rainmakers, officiating elders, chiefs and kings). Every person is by nature religious; where the individual is, there is his religion, for he is a religious being. But the changes brought by Western Christianity have disturbed or broken down traditional religious meanings, structures, and traditions, leaving people confused, with little or no religious foundation or spirit. The African Independent Churches attempt to restore what has been lost. Often this restoration results in the destruction of implanted mainline Christian structures. For example, in South Africa, apartheid was an infamous characteristic of Christianity. The AIC movement destroyed that vestige of Christianity.

Almost all African Independent Churches trace their origins from Anglican-Protestant churches; emphasize the Bible, and the importance of a personal relationship with Jesus Christ. Few AIC denominations derive from Roman Catholic or Orthodox roots, traditionally inextricably focused on church unity and loyalty to the Roman church or patriarch. AICs are essentially spiritual religious movements, rather than social, political or economic reactions to societal problems. The AICs are a protest movement, not to reject Christianity but to Africanize Christianity. From another perspective, the establishment of AICs has been an attempt by the African people to localize the church, to incarnate the church in the deepest theological sense, in which the word becomes flesh in the culture of the present. This effort requires both openness to African cultures and comparing African ways to Gospel values, with the goal of mutual purification and enrichment.

Professor John Mbiti, a universally recognized East African theologian, refers to this need to incarnate and localize the African church. He writes about a new "crisis in mission" confronting Christianity in Africa. He postulates three challenges which Christianity must confront in the next thirty to fifty years.

First, Christianity must be made relevant to the lives and affairs of the continent; it must adapt or perish. Accommodating African traditions will gain for it cultural relevance. Identifying more completely with African aspirations will equal its practical relevance. Secondly, Christianity must be Africanized, not only in personnel, but in such things as structure, theology, worship, and carrying out its mission.[22] To transplant prefabricated Christianity from Berkeley to Nairobi will not suffice. The African church must produce a Christianity which bears the imprint of having been brewed in an African pot: made in Africa, by Africa and for Africa. Finally, this Christianity must be mission-oriented to carry out its task of proclaiming the Gospel. Many concerned scholars question the collaborative capacity of the historic missionary churches and the AICs, and in doing so give meaning and purpose to a widely expressed desire for dialogue.

Roman Catholicism Rising to the Challenge

The African Catholic bishops initiated a response to this crisis in mission at the 1994 Synod of bishops in Rome. Mbiti writes, "It would be only at the African bishop's Synod in Rome, 1994, that inculturation began to make headway under pressure from the African bishops."[23] The bishops acknowledged that the continent is full of bad news the continent that it is plagued by abject poverty, catastrophic mismanagement of available inadequate resources, political instability and social disorientation. Such hegemony is dehumanizing, distorting humanity.

The late Julius Nyerere, described these problems several years ago:

> We say that humanity was created in the image of God. I refuse to imagine a God who is poor, ignorant, and fearful, oppressed, wretched-which is the lot of the majority he created in his own image and likeness. Human beings are creators of themselves and of their conditions. Under the present conditions we are creatures not of God, but of our fellow human beings.[24]

The African Synod made special note of the roles of religious leaders and the laity, collaborating with other people of good will, in mastering these problems. The synod's work sessions were structured around five themes: proclamation, inculturation, dialogue, justice and peace, and communications, with chief emphasis being on inculturation, and making the church more genuinely African. The Coptic church of Ethiopia and Egypt was cited by the synod as a role model for the Roman church in addressing inculturation.

As acknowledged by the Synod, a major issue in the synergetic process is the status of African traditional marriage, which is ubiquitously polygamous. Polygamy is a universal custom in Africa. The church, however, demands that those who wish to be Christians send away all their wives, except the first. Baptism is not offered to the additional wives unless they agree to separate from their husband. Because of this teaching and discipline, great numbers of Christians are excluded from the sacraments. This is a long-standing and unresolved problem, seriously compromising the unity and strength of the church.

Inculturation and Islam

Some scholars suggest that the African Christian church might learn from the Islamic community's acculturative history and methods. Like Christianity, Islam came to Africa loaded with culturally biased expectations and institutions. But Islam did not land on empty ground. It found African people deeply immersed in their own traditions. The encounter between Islam and Africa resulted in at least some cultural synthesis, producing what Leopold Sedar Senghor poet, statesman and former president of the Republic of Senegal called "half-caste cultures."

For centuries, Islam did not challenge Christianity south of the Sahara. But today it is awakening. Some Christian leaders are reacting aggressively out of fear. Perhaps, through Christian-Islamic dialogue, the problems of inculturation can be effectively addressed. The Christian church can learn from the Islamic community.

Conclusion

The current relationship between African Traditional Religions, Islam, and Christianity is marked by struggle and dissension, but also by growth and hope. The struggle is for the soul of Africa. All three traditions are contending with Western secularism. Continued dissension threatens to de-Africanize Africa; however, in this religious, political, and economic conflict are abundant opportunities for mutual enrichment. Collaboratively, they could affect secularism for the social, economic and political welfare of Africa. The challenge to African Traditional Religions, Christianity and Islam is to find a way to connect, to share the true, the good, and the beautiful enshrined in each of them.

Adinkra Symbol for Unity and Diversity

CHAPTER V

The Lion Speaks Words of Wisdom...
Dialogue: The Challenge to Christianity,
Islam and African Traditional Religions

An ancient and famous Chinese proverb declares, "a journey of one thousand *li* (miles) begins with one step."[1] Not by leaps and bounds, but step by step—so must go the dialogue between Christianity, Islam and African Traditional Religions. The conflicts of the past must make way for cooperation. In this infinitely divided world, whoever can build a bridge between peoples must be encouraged.

To suggest dialogue presupposes disagreement between groups of people, and offers a solution, as an instrument for the understanding of meanings, values and attitudes. Inherent in such collaborative action is the need for courage and humility: the courage to take risks, and the humility to accept the possibility of undergoing a change in oneself.[2]

In the case of Islam versus Christianity, the causes of conflict or disagreement recall the very birth of Islam in the seventh century C.E., and are characterized by prejudice, differences of language and imagery, contrary purposes, anxieties, defensiveness and lust for power; despite Christianity and Islam's common doctrine of the golden rule which calls individuals to live together in harmony. "Do for others what you want them to do for you; this is the meaning of the Law of Moses and the teachings of the prophets."[3] "No one of you is a believer until he loves for his brother that which he loves for himself."[4]

This chapter turns to the current need for paths to understanding between Christians and Muslims, examining areas of conflict, common heritage, and practical steps towards effective dialogue.

Sources of Disagreement

The characteristic feature of the self-understanding of any principle, whether religious or secular, is that its own constitutive beliefs are uniquely and fully true, while the convictions of those outside its pale are entirely, or at least defectively, false. Claiming truth for one's own belief system to the exclusion of all others deeply troubles African societies today; however, religious beliefs and theological differences are usually not the main causes of conflict. Normally, conflicts arise from racial, economic, political and cultural factors. Religion often colors such discords or intensifies them, or is used to foster divisions and conflict.

Theological Hindrances to Dialogue

Many obstacles to Muslim-Christian harmony are deeply rooted in each faith's negative, reciprocated attitudes toward the other. Consider common Islamic attitudes toward Christianity.

Islam's encounter with Christianity remains to this day a mix of misunderstanding, mutual accusations and bitter polemical exchange. The major source of this sad state of affairs is obvious: Islam claims to be in the same prophetic line as Judaism and Christianity, but superior to both; a claim considered heretical by Christians. Similarly antagonistic is the Muslim view of Christianity as a distortion of Islam; for Christians call Jesus the son of God. According to the Qur'an, Jesus was a distinguished prophet, but not a divine being. Muslims believe in the virgin birth of Jesus and his distinctiveness, but they do not grant him superiority among the prophets or believe him to be the son of God. That kind of association with God would be a violation of *Tahwid* (the unity of God). The declaration that Allah has no son constitutes the essential difference between Islam and Christianity. The Holy Qur'an is careful in every instance to call Jesus the son of Mary.

Islam allows that Jesus may be a son of God in the metaphorical sense, as each of us may be if we obey and believe in one God.[5] As a matter of fact, the Holy Qur'an warns Christians in these words:

> People of the Book, *ahl-kitab*, go not beyond the bounds in your religion, and say not as to God, but the truth. The Messiah, Jesus son of Mary, was only the Messenger of God, and his word, that he committed to Mary, and a spirit from him. So believe in God and His Messengers and say not, Three. Refrain, better is it for you. God is only one God. Glory is to Him, that He should have a son! (Sura 4:169).

According to the Qur'an, Jesus was born miraculously of Mary. Instead of death on the cross, Muslims believe he was miraculously taken back to heaven before his death. Along with its refutation of Jesus' divinity, death and resurrection, Islam rejects of the doctrine of original sin. To a Muslim, sin is forgetfulness and salvation is remembrance. Therefore, Muslims pray five times a day, to remember Allah and his commands.

At the same time, the word "salvation" is not found in the Holy Qur'an, and is a word seldom used by Muslims. Followers of Islam speak rather of success in achieving paradise.[6] Success depends on sincere faith, righteous work and God's mercy (Qur'an 48:29). Examples of such good deeds are visiting the sick, clothing the naked and feeding the hungry.

According to the Holy Qur'an, Jesus prophesied the coming of the messenger among the gentiles, who would complete God's favor on mankind (Qur'an 7: 61:6). But it is thought that over time, Christians and Jews distorted their own scriptures as an excuse to avoid the acceptance of Muhammad and Islam. According to Islamic teaching, Abraham was a true Muslim, Jesus was a true Muslim, and true faith can only be found in Islam. The Holy Qur'an says, "They are non-believers who say God is the third of the three. No God is there but one God" (Sura 5:78). Such statements offend most Christians. Naturally,

Christians resent this interpretation, since it effectively dispossesses them of their faithful heritage (i.e. the Trinity) by outsiders who claim, with irritatingly routine conviction, that genuine Christianity is found only in Islam.

Theoretically, were Muslims and Christians to exchange ideas about these theological issues, Muslims would not be required to believe in the Christian doctrines of Jesus' divine nature or original sin. The Muslim would be called to respect, not to accept, such Christian teaching.

Christian Perceptions of Islam

For generations, Christians have treated Islam as unstudied and "lacking in originality."[7] Such analysis suggests that Islam is a false religion, deliberately perverting the truth. Christianity insists that Islam simply derives its inspiration from Judeo-Christian traditions, but Muslims disagree and maintain that the Qur'an is God's revelation to Muhammad. For Muslims, Islam's scripture is literally God's word, without Christian or Jewish influence. Further complicating matters, Christianity does not regard Muhammad as an authentic prophet. For Christians, all prophecy ceased with the coming of Jesus. Muhammad came only after the time of prophecy.

All Muslims are united by a simple confession of faith: "There is no god but God, and Muhammad is his Prophet." That statement is the first of the five pillars of Muslim belief. The remaining four are prayer, almsgiving, fasting and pilgrimage to Mecca (the holy city of Islam.) All five pillars of Islam were taught and practiced by the Prophet himself, and his exemplary life came to be known as the Sunna and the Hadith. They comprise the practices and sayings of the Prophet, and are second in authority only to the Qur'an.

Historical Causes of Christian-Muslim Conflict

The first great Muslim expansion into Christian territories began in 634 C.E., shortly after the death of the Prophet, into Syria, and then Egypt, North Africa, Spain, Sicily and the kingdom of Jerusalem. Christendom's response to Islam took two forms: the struggle to regain control of Spain (the Reconquista, 1000-1492), and Italy and Sicily (1061), and a series of Christian wars, the Crusades (1095-1453).[8]

These military conflicts over the course of eight centuries stoked the fires of Christian/Islamic anger and resentment.

In more modern times, the colonization of Muslim countries by European and American nations poured salt on old wounds. Today, the incursion into Iraq and the burgeoning Muslim population growth in Europe and Asia is tearing open these old wounds. Mutual suspicion and hostility remains today, a festering sore. These very real, very bloody events of yesterday and today must be understood in order for future fraternal efforts to be realistic and productive.

Conflict but Commonalities

The Swahili people of East Africa have a proverb, *Wapiganapo tembo, nyasi huumia,* which means, "Where elephants fight, the grass gets hurt." In the African struggle between Islam and Christianity, it is Africa that has been hurt. The traditional cultures of African people continue to be harmed, in the villages and in the slums, in politics and in economic life. However, despite their differences, Christians and Muslims have much in common. They believe in one God, the creator and provider, the merciful, compassionate and final judge of humanity. "The Abrahamic faith in monotheism unites Judaism, Christianity, and Islam as consecutive articulations of trust in God."[9] Abraham is their common father-in-faith.

The honor and respect which Muslims have for Mary and Jesus constitute a unique bond which Christians do not have with any other religious group. "Mary, the mother of Jesus is the only woman in the Qur'an called by her proper name. All other women in the Qur'an are identified by their relationship to a man."[10] Mary is mentioned nineteen times in the Bible, but thirty-four times in the Qur'an, wherein she is called the greatest of all women.[11]

Given these commonalities, opportunities for connection exist. Prompted by their shared experience of painful conflict, and their common desire for peace, Muslims and Christians are beginning to realize that the time is ripe for dialogue, for exploring one another's culture and common heritage, absent any desire to prove that one is true and the other not. Disagreements may continue, but must be tempered with authentic attempts to bridge their differences.

Building Bridges

Successful dialogue will take place between persons of different faith perspectives, but not only between the bureaucratic representatives of faith systems. That is to say, it must be a living experience of men and women encountering each other within the structure of their own theological positions, not as deep-rooted defenders of particular systems, but as people of continually maturing faiths. Dialogue implies more than discussion, but an attitude, a spirit of friendship, a wish to meet the other while remaining true to one's own faith. Sometimes the best witness is one who is ready to listen. Those engaging each other for mutual benefit will set aside what separates them and concentrate on what will foster unity and friendship.

Types of Dialogue

In essence, there are six kinds of dialogue: parliamentary, institutional, theological, dialogue in community, spiritual, and inner dialogue. In view of the current situation in Africa, it is not necessary to engage in parliamentary, institutional or theological dialogue, debating points of conflict such as the Trinity, the Vatican, the Qur'an, or Mecca. First things must come first. Successful efforts for the betterment of Africa will be founded at the level of the community; in other words, with regard to pressing communal issues involving quality of life, such as the continent's six million refugees and displaced persons, the uprooted, the starving, those bereft of land, family, friends and the future.

The African Community in Dialogue

In Africa, community forums include market places, street corners, times of festivals or holy days, during the course of civil or humanitarian projects, and at times of community togetherness or family crisis. People in the community think and talk together about common concerns, such as violence, militarism, or economic depression; they think and talk about the marriages of their children, and the community's responsibility towards the elderly. On such common ground, the African, be he Christian, Muslim or traditionalist, can initiate a discourse that will effectively meet the challenges Africans now face. Ironically, little productive exchange of ideas occurs when two or more academics, ecclesiastics, or politicians sit around a table with the express purpose of getting somewhere; however, positive sustainable change in Africa requires that both formal and informal types of community dialogue be established.

Times, Places, Circumstances for Dialogue

In Islam, Christianity, and traditional cultures, there are holy days and events that could be rich opportunities for bridging cultural differences. For example, *Idi el fitr,* the festival at the end of Ramadan, *Id el haj,* the festival in commemoration of Muhammad's journey to Mecca, and *Maulidi Day,* celebration of Prophet Muhammad's birthday, are the most significant Muslim public holy days. The most significant Christian holy days are Good Friday, Easter, and Christmas, celebrating the death, resurrection, and birth of Jesus, respectively.

For purposes of creating friendships, these Islamic and Christian holy days could be celebrated by the entire African community. Public policy, the laws of local and national governments, could foster greater religious freedom and encourage the ecumenical spirit among citizens. Cooperation among the religious communities could manifest itself, for example, by people helping each other build churches and mosques. Imams might invite Christian priests and ministers to talk about the community's concern for the poor; in turn, they might teach in Christian churches about other community concerns for the poor and the elderly. Members of each religious community could promote an interfaith dialogue by attending each other's religious ceremonies, such as rites of passage, weddings, and funeral services. In recent years, the people of Tanzania have successfully modeled such communal and ecumenical efforts for all of Africa.

African Traditional Religions and Dialogue

Among members of African Traditional Religions, marriage is the centerpiece of communal existence. Through the rituals and events of marriage, all dimensions of life and death and time come into focus. In the traditional view of life, the entire drama of "sasa and zamani" is realized in the marriage, as members of the community encounter the departed and those yet to be born. For African traditionalists, the effects of death are reduced or neutralized by marriage and family life. The inevitable aspects of marriage, such as childbearing, guarantee human, tribal and individual survival. Effectively, death is conquered by marriage; those who participate in and celebrate marriage come together to share life, with all its joy, suffering and hope. Participation in community marriage celebrations marks a person as a promoter of life. It is at this point, at this time and place, that the community effort needed to heal Africa's wounds would be very appropriately launched. Muslims, Christians and traditionalists could interact, build community and become one in mind and heart.

At Times of Death and Burial

Traditional religious ceremonies of death and burial present another possibility. Tribal expectation is that regardless of creed, one is expected to join in mourning the dead. Failure to do so implicates one in a person's death. In many Christian and Muslim families, the home of a recently deceased person is a holy place where people, regardless of religious creed, pray and read from the scriptures, both the holy Bible and the holy Qur'an. During that time, religious leaders' family members from the clan and friends might preach. This common human experience is another rich opportunity for the building of friendships and community.

African Dialogue: Promotion of Human Rights

There is abundant, fertile common ground in the religious communities of Africa on which to base fruitful inter-religious dialogue. Massive social and economic challenges are confronting all Africans, without deference to creed or culture. These challenges would yield to a genuine struggle for peace between African Traditional Religions, Islam and Christianity.

The widespread violation of human rights concerns all of Africa. The author is convinced that the best chance for successful African inter-religious interchange would primarily focus on the restoration and promotion of human rights. Africa's crises need to be addressed in the context of human rights.

A human right—the claim to freely choose and perform an action which a person judges necessary for life, liberty and the pursuit of happiness—is not a favor or privilege bestowed along with citizenship, or the gift of a benevolent authority. Human rights are rooted in and flow from the equal dignity of all human beings, the brotherhood of all, without exception or condition, regardless of race, color, creed, age, gender, sexual orientation or political allegiance.

In their 1994 open letter to President Moi of Kenya, the Catholic bishops of Kenya decried the extensive violation of human rights in Kenya which they believed to be so extensive that "most people do not believe there is any law or order left in Kenya."[12] The bishops continued that people of all walks of life and religious traditions should labor together in harvesting justice and peace, and that African religious and secular leaders should walk together in humankind's long march for freedom, democracy and human rights.

Nonviolence and African Dialogue

Another forum for inter-religious dialogue in Africa is the universally recognized aspiration to resolve social problems by non-violent means. With the exception of extremist elements in Islam, Christianity and African Traditional Religions, the desire for peace and justice as fruits of non-violent community dialogue lies deep in the hearts of the African people, as in all human beings. Dr. Martin Luther King, Jr. voiced this universal, heartfelt desire:

> We shall match your capacity to inflict suffering by our capacity to endure suffering. We will meet your physical force with soul force. Do to us what you will and we will still love you. We cannot in all good conscience obey your unjust laws and abide by an unjust system, because non-cooperation with evil is as much a moral obligation as is cooperation with good, and so throw us in jail and we will still love you. Send your hooded perpetrators of violence into our communities at the midnight hour and drag us out on some way road and leave us half dead as you beat us, and we will still love you...be assured that we will wear you down by our capacity to suffer, and one day we will win our freedom. We will not only win freedom for ourselves, we will so appeal to your heart and conscience that we will win you in the process, and our victory will be a double victory.[13]

Dr. King frequently recalled that the perpetrators of abuses were his brothers and sisters. But he was a man of Christian faith, committed even unto death to non-violence. The example of his life provides continued encouragement for peace-seeking people everywhere.

Mohandas Gandhi: Inspiration for Africa

The same striving for peace and justice through only non-violent means is echoed in the words of Mohandas Gandhi:

So far as I can see, the atomic bomb has deadened the finest feeling that has sustained humanity for ages. There used to be so called laws of war which made it intolerable. Now we know the naked truth. War knows no law except that of might. The atom bomb brought an empty victory to the allied armies, but it resulted for the time being in destroying the soul of Japan. What has happened to the soul of the destroying nation is yet too early to see.[14]

Like King, Gandhi died violently at the hands of an assassin, but the struggle and his spirit of non-violence continues. The devout Indian Hindu continues to inspire African people in their struggle for the soul of Africa.

Conclusion

War, injustice, dissension, and failure define the world in which modern Africans live. But these oppressive circumstances brim with opportunities for Christianity, Islam and African Traditional Religions to establish authentic inter-religious dialogue, such that would make heard the voices of the voiceless. Their abundant common ground would surely yield the fruits of peace and justice for all in the African heartland. Any efforts toward collaborative improvement must be communally based, and not confined to meetings of religious or community leaders, or scholars or politicians. African nations might be known not only as part of the developing Third World, but a Third World spiritual force modeling religious reconciliation. The Lion of Africa's belief is that African traditionalists, Christians and Muslims, men and women of boundless good will, are prepared to open the channels of understanding and become a light to the nations.

Reflections

As only a native son can, the author has remembered the past, described the present and imagined the future of the historical confluence in Africa of African Traditional Religions, Islam, Christianity and Secularism. This coming together has its consequences in conflict. Africa is at war. But the Lion of Africa finds hope in this conflict, and great promise for the people of Africa.

African Traditional Religions have deep roots in the tree of life that is modern Africa. Understanding the story of its spirituality, enshrined in its culture, languages, religious beliefs, rituals and art, will facilitate the scholar's understanding and deepen his reverence for African people. Simultaneously, such understanding and reverence will surely aid in the resolution of African conflicts and facilitate the appropriate inculturation of Islam, Christianity and African Traditional Religions.

Christianity's failure to receive African culture meant its failed first attempt to evangelize the African continent north of the Sahara, a failure exacerbated by the militant expansion of Islam. A second attempt by the Christian church to evangelize took place in sub-Saharan Africa. This missionary effort was seriously compromised because Christianity came packaged in the trappings of Western economic and political colonialism, as well as the sectarian divisiveness born of the European Protestant Reformation.

The third phase of African evangelization has met with more success. But, continued debate concerning inculturation hinders Christianity's growth in Africa, while supporting the growth of African Independent churches.

Islam first came to northern Africa in the mid-seventh century. Military conquests, and the Islamization and Arabization of the indigenous population displaced both African Traditional Religions and nascent Christianity. In later centuries, Islam expanded through commerce and trade into sub-Saharan Africa. In parts of the continent, Islam has been generally synthesized with African Traditional Religions, aided by its identification with the anti-colonial spirit of the African people. For many, Islam is perceived as offering more in life than foreign, colonial Christianity and culture.

The current relationship in Africa of its major religious divisions is marked not only by struggle, rivalry, suspicion and dissension, but also by signs of reconciliation. All its religious heritages are contending with Western-exported materialistic secularism. At issue is the very soul of Africa. Forces are at work which could de-Africanize Africa.

In all of these conflicts and crises exist abundant opportunities for positive change. African Traditional Religions, Christianity and Islam could engage in mutually enriching fraternal efforts, possibly lessening the power of secularism for the social, economic and political welfare of Africa. However, many concerned scholars are questioning the ability and the willingness of the missionary churches and those practicing African Traditional Religions to collaborate.

The voices of the silenced and voiceless Africa demand to be heard. Many are the avenues for such expression, particularly in the community celebrations and rituals of the three religious traditions. Their mutual concern and present efforts in regard to the restoration and promotion of human rights, as well as their shared desire to resolve social problems by non-violent means, could be the optimum starting point for successful collaboration and the transformation of Africa.

Points for Discussion

- Inculturation/contextualization demands a thorough understanding and reverence for the roots and the present manifestations of a people's culture.

- Modern day Western culture, largely expressed by materialism and secularism, gravely threatens a loss of identity for Africans.

- African Traditional Religions, Christianity, and Islam seem to be competing for the soul of Africa. If the competition continues, the losers will be the suffering people of Africa.

- Any imported religion in Africa must be cultivated in the African culture.

- No one will take seriously a theology which preaches the need for inculturation, but simply ignores the all-encompassing social misery in Africa.

- Western scholarship has not completely abandoned its outdated view of Africa. To the West, the world is still divided into the civilized West and the primitive non-Western world, now politely referred to as the developing countries.

- A hold-over from brutally racist times: "Africans have empty heads and uncommitted souls."

- Dialogue has to be in one voice: To oppress the poor is to insult the Creator" (Proverbs 14:31).

- "The split between the Gospel and the culture is without a doubt the drama of our time. Therefore, every effort must be made to ensure a full evangelization of culture, or more correctly, of cultures. They have to be regenerated by an encounter with the Gospel" (Pope Paul VI).

Notes

Prologue

[1] David Shannon, "An Anti-Bellum Sermon: Resources for African-American Hermeneutics," Cain Hope Ed. <u>Stony The Road We Trod</u>: African American Biblical Interpretation, (Fortress, 1991), 98.

[2] Chinua Achebe, *Anthills of the Savannah* (Anchor Press Doubleday: New York, 1988), 114.

Chapter One – Confluence of African Religions

[1] Okot P'Bitek, *African Religions in Western Scholarship* (Kampala, Uganda Literature Bureau, 1980), 88.

[2] John Mbiti, *African and Religions Philosophy* (London: Oxford University Press, 1969), 24.

[3] P'Bitek, 109.

[4] John Mbiti, *African Religions and Philosophy* (London: Oxford University Press, 1969), 24.

[5] Geoffrey Parrinder, *African Mythology* (New York: Peter Bedrick Books, 1986), 44.

Chapter Two - Christianity in Africa

[1] J. Mbiti, 230.

[2] Ali Mazrui, *The Africans* (New York: Praeger Publishers, 1986), 69.

[3] Jomo Kenyatta as quoted in Ali Mazrui, *Cultural Forces in World Politics* (Nairobi: Heinemann, 1990), 6.

[4] Joseph, G. Donders, *Non-Bourgeois Theology* (New York: Orbis Books, 1985), 2

[5] J. Mbiti, 232.

[6] Justin S. Ukpong, *African Theologies: Now-A Profile* (Eldoret, Kenya: Gaba Publications, 1984), 8.

[7] Ibid., 8-9.

[8] Ibid, 9.

[9] J. Donders, 2.

Chapter Three – Islam in Africa

[1] John L. Esposto, *Islam: The straight Path* (New York: Oxford University Press, 1988), 49.

[2] Ibid., 50.

Chapter Four – Major African Religious and Cultural Conflicts

[1] Ali A. Mazrui, *The Africans: A Triple Heritage* (Toronto: Little Brown and Company, 1986), 11.

[2] Ibid., 112.

[3] Ibid., 202.

[4] S.C. Neill, *A History of Christian Missions* (London: Penguin Books, 1964), 494.

[5] Ibid., 495

[6] Ali A. Mazrui, *The Africans* (New York: Praeger Publishers, 1986), 146.

[7] Benezet Bujo, *African Theology in Its Social Context* (New York: Orbis Books, 1992), 44.

[8] Jean-Marc Ela, *My Faith as an African* (Acton Publishers, Nairobi: 2001), xiii.

[9] Pope Paul VI, Apostolic Exhortation *Evangilii Nuntiandi* (December 8, 1995), no. 20.

[10] The "Tasks of Special Synod for Africa, "Origins 23 (April 21, 1994): 766.

[11] Elizabeth Isichei, *A history of Christianity in Africa*, (New Jersey: World Press Lawrenceville, 1994),114.

[12] Ibid., 114.

[13] Jomo Kenyatta, *Facing Mount Kenya* (New York: Vintage Books, 1965), 258.

[14] Ibid., 259.

[15] Ibid., 259.

[16] Ibid., 260.

[17] Walbert Bulhmann, *The Missions on Trial* (New York: Orbis Books, 1979), 32.

[18] Ibid., 32.

[19] Ralph, Martin, *The Catholic Church at the End of the Age* (San Francisco: Ignatius Press, 1994), 63.

[20] Gerald G. Brown, *Christian Response to Change in East African Traditional Societies* (London: Wood Brooke College, 1973), 37.

[21] Mugambi, J.N.K. *African Heritage and Contemporary Christianity*, (Nairobi: Longman, 1989), 88.

[22] Tad Szulc, *Pope John Paul II: The Biography* (New York: Scribner, 1995), 340.

[23] "The Tasks of the Special Synod for Africa," *Origins* 23 (April 21, 1994):762.

[24] Julius Nyerere as quoted in George Kinoti, "African Christians and the Future of Africa," *Transformation* Vol. 11 (July-September, 1994), 25.

Chapter Five – Dialogue: The Challenge to Christianity, Islam, and African Traditional Religions

[1] Lao-tze as quoted in Charles Kimball, *String Together: A Way Forward in Christian-Muslim Relations* (New York: Orbis Books, 1991), 37.

[2] Aylward Shorter, *African Christian Theology-Adaptation or Incarnation?* (Great Britain: Northumberland Press, 1975), 5.

[3] Matthew 7:12

[4] Francis Arinze, *Church in Dialogue* (San Francisco: Saint Ignatius Press, 1990), 255.

[5] Ira G. Zepp, Jr. *A Muslim Primer* (Westminster Maryland: Wakefield Editions, 1992), 225.

[6] Ibid., 96.

[7] Hans Kung, *Christianity and the World Religions* (New York: Double-day and Co., 1986), 25.

[8] John L. Esposito, *Islam: The Straight Path* (New York: Oxford University Press, 1991), 59.

[9] Hans Kung and Jurgen Moltmann, *Islam: A Challenge for Christianity* (London: SCM Press, 1994), 106.

[10] Ira G. Zepp., Jr. 225.

[11] Arinze Francis, 315.

[12] *Africa*, Bishops Open Letter to President Moi, March, 1994, 16.

[13] Martin Luther King, Jr., in John Dear, *Disarming the Heart* (Waterloo, Ontario: Herald Press, 1993), 55.

[14] Mohandas Ghandi, as quoted in Thomas Merton, *Ghandi on Non-Violence* (New York: New Directions Publishing,1965), 32.

Bibliography

Aylward, Shorter. *African Christian Theology-Adaptation or Incarnation?* Great Britain: Northumberland Press, 1975.

Bujo, Benezet. *African Theology in Its Social Context.* Maryknoll, New York: Orbis Books, 992.

Lao-tze as quoted in Charles, Kimball, *String Together: A Way Forward in Christian-Muslim Relations.* New York: Orbis Books, 1991.

David, Shannon. "An Anti-Bellum Sermon: Resource for African-American Hermeneutics," Cain Hope Ed. *Stony The Road We Trod:* African-American Biblical Interpretation, Fortress, 1991.

Dear, John. *Disarming the Heart.* Waterloo, Ontario: Herald Press, 1993.

Donders, G. Joseph. *Praying and Preaching the Sunday Gospel,* Maryknoll, NY: Orbis Books, 1990.

Elizabeth, Isichei. *A History of Christianity in Africa,* Lawrenceville, New Jersey: World Press, 1995.

Francis, Arinze. *Church in Dialogue.* San Francisco: Saint Ignatius Press, 1990.

Geoffrey, Parrinder. *African Mythology.* New York: Peter Bedrick Books, 1986.

George, Kinoti. "African Christians and the future of Africa," *Transformation Vol. 11*(July-September, 1994) 25.

Hans Kung and Jurgen, Moltmann. *Islam: A Challenge for Christianity,* London: SCM Press, 1994.

Iran G. Zepp, Jr. *A Muslim Primer.* Westminster Maryland: Wakefield Editions, 1992.

Jean-Marc Ela. *My Faith as an African,* Nairobi: Acton Publishers, 2001.

John, Esposito. *Islam: The Straight Path,* New York: Oxford University Press, 1991.

Jomo, Kenyatta. *Facing Mount Kenya,* New York: Vintage Books, 1965.

Justin S. Ukpong. *African Theologies: Now-A Profile* Eldoret, Kenya: Gaba Publications, 1984.

Mazrui, A. Ali. *Cultural Forces in World Politics.* Nairobi: Heinemann, 1990.

— *The Africans: A Triple Heritage.* Boston, MA: Little Brown and Co., 1986.

Mbiti, John. *The Concepts of God in Africa.* London: SPCK, 1970.
—*African Religions and Philosophy.* Nairobi: Heinemann Press, 1980.

Merton, Thomas. *Ghandhi on Non-Violence.* New York: New Directions Publishing, 1965.

p'Bitek, Okot. *African Religions in Western Scholarship.* Kampala: Uganda Literature Bureau, 1990.

Pope Paul VI. Apostolic Exhortation *Evangili Nutiandi, (December 8, 1995), no. 20.*

Ralph, Martin. *The Catholic Church at the End of the Age,* San Francisco: Ignatius Press, 1994.

S.C. Neil. *A History of Christian Missions,* London: Penguin Books, 1964.

Tad Szulc. *Pope John Paul II: The Biography,* New York: Scribner, 1995.

The Tasks of the Special Synod for Africa, "*Origins* 23 (April 21, 1994), 766.

Walbert, Bulhmann. *The Missions on Trial,* New York: Orbis Books, 1979.

Index

A

LaVergne, TN USA
04 January 2010
168712LV00007B/6/A